Love of Life

Love of Life

A BROOKLYN GIRL'S STORY

NANCY SAPARATA SABATINO

Full Court Press
Englewood Cliffs, New Jersey

First Edition

Published in the United States of America
by Full Court Press, 601 Palisade Avenue,
Englewood Cliffs, NJ 07632
fullcourtpress.com

ISBN 978-1-946989-83-3
Library of Congress Control No. 2020924904

Editing and book design by Barry Sheinkopf

For Peter,
Alexander, Joseph, and Michael
Thank you for all the years
of happiness you've given me

I

BEGINNINGS

THE LIGHTS WERE DIM, and I could only see shadows, but I felt a sense of warmth and peace around me. I was an infant in a bassinet. I do not remember the words my parents spoke, only the fact that I had such a wondrous feeling of love and security. I have managed, somehow or other, to preserve that feeling to this day.

As an Italian girl growing up in Brooklyn, I know I had an extremely adventurous and interesting life. Looking back at my seventy-eight years, I recall a crowded array of incidents that were instrumental in forming the person I am today.

"Daddy, Daddy! Please make the big black dog go away!" There I was, at three years old, lying in bed when all of a sudden a gigantic black dog was sitting on the foot of it, staring straight at me. I can still feel the terror of wondering when he would attack. Of course, as he always did, my father comforted me, saying it was only a dream, that I should fall asleep again.

At the age of eight, my two favorite cousins were Provie and Lenny. We spent many holidays together and lived only four houses apart. In those days aunts, uncles, cousins, and grandparents were all, for the most part, within walking distance of one another. I loved walking to see my family, being able to simply ring a bell and always find someone there. My grandmother would say, "Come in! Have some Italian bread dipped in coffee." It's a deep satisfaction to have memories of such insignificant moments.

Having been born on Decoration Day, 1942, I was one of many war babies. It did keep my father out of the army. I continued to have a strong feeling of security knowing that my mother and father were there whenever I needed them.

And I can understand, looking back at my childhood experiences, why I am the person I am today. I was a free spirit, given the opportunity by my parents to explore the dance of life.

At the ripe old age of eight, for example, I set sail on a voyage up the Hudson River. We started our adventure from an inlet of the main river in the town of Catskill. My cousins Provie, age eight, and Peter, age five, were my shipmates. We embarked on a journey that was to end very uncomfortably for the three of us.

It took us an hour to row to a duck house on the Hudson. We had brought candles, wallpaper, cookies, and other essential supplies. We remained inside that little house for many hours, not realizing that the tide was going out.

Then I looked out the window and yelled in horror because the boat was now on a tremendously long sandbar. We had no shoes and had to drag it, while the needle-like surface made our feet bleed. Darkness was setting in too, and the wind began to chill our half-naked bodies.

When we finally got the boat into the middle of the river, the Coast Guard came. *Gee whiz,* I thought, *why couldn't they have gotten here when we really needed them?* They towed our boat home, and our fathers tanned our little hides very well for giving them such a fright.

I've often thought about my father's furious reaction, even went so far as to write a letter to him (which I didn't send):

> *Dear Dad,*
>
> *I cannot understand that, after all these years, you finally admitted to me that we are so much alike. It was wrong of you to punish me so severely for something I did as a child, when you*

did something similar and didn't see any harm in it. I'm referring to the time you swam out to the buoy at Coney Island, only to find that the tide had changed, leaving you hanging onto a large piece of metal for hours.

You were a daring teenager who didn't think of the people on the beach distraught at the thought that, they were convinced, you had drowned. If you had taken into consideration that the reason you were swimming out so far in such a short time had to do with the tides, you'd have realized how difficult it would be to return. Of course you were young at the time and didn't think that far ahead. You lived for the moment, never considering the consequences of your action.

But if you feel that what you did was not so terrible, why was I given such a bad whipping when my small boat got stuck on a sandbar in the Hudson River when I was eight years old?

I realize that my actions were misguided because I never considered that the Hudson River was like an ocean with respect to the tides. When my boat was wedged in the mud, I knew I would never be able to make it back to the house before dark. I feared the consequences of my being late, since I knew we had to drive back from the Catskills to New York City.

Now that I realize you did something so similar to what I did, you should have understood. Why then did you think it was right to reprimand me with a spanking instead of talking?

This boating incident didn't dampen our spirits, though, because we went on to have many more adventures. Providence and I decided to take the boat across the river to a metals factory. While we were there, we collected pails of metal shavings and filled up the whole boat. Then, to our dismay, on the journey back across the river, the boat sank! Still, once my parents realized that I was a miniature Lewis and Clark, they gave me pretty much free reign to travel where I wanted. The swamp was a beautiful place to wander into. The large skunk plants and towering ferns gave me at once feelings of excitement and fright.

We found a spot deep in that swamp with a beautiful little patch of green grass. We lay down there and told each other all our inner feelings. It was our very own special, private place where no one could find us—an escape from the real world in the Catskill Mountains.

My cousins meant everything to me. We had so many adventures, so much fun, together. Little kids do enjoy doing silly things. We would, for example, have nudie parties: Three girls, and three boys, would have to show their private parts. Luckily, at eight, you don't have much to show. We promised we would do it again when we grew up—but of course we never did!

Another day with the Catskill cousins, we visited an abandoned house. It was small, so we decided to demolish it. First, the beams that held up the porch came down. Then we removed all the walls. After that, the rest started to collapse. End of house.

My cousins' Catskill home had been built in 1726 by the Dubois family. It had about twenty rooms and a large wraparound porch. There was also a steepled carport attached to the main house. Running around the roof there was dangerous, but it was also lots of fun. We climbed mountains and traveled to a waterfall to collect clay and make vases and ash trays to dry in the sun. We had a beautiful gazebo on the property to work in.

During that period, I also spent a great deal of my young life in a small town in New Jersey, where I met Carol and Janet, who became my best summer friends. The three of us did everything together. We built a small wooden cage deep in the woods and ran around in it like little Indians. We also built many forts in and around the trees in the woods. When our older brothers located the forts, they usually destroyed them.

The railroad tracks were another great place to play. It was especially exciting when we were on the train trestle and the train came round the bend. Mountain climbing always gave us a great deal of pleasure when we were at a loss for something to do. Swimming in the Ramapo River, and swinging from ropes tied to the trees, gave me a taste of the life I thought Tom Sawyer must have had.

When I was a kid, most of my summers were spent in Oakland, New Jersey. My cousin Lenny and I did some nasty things to the Dugan's man. He delivered cakes and cookies to my Mom. Because of what we did, he never came to our house again. Everyone in our family wanted to know what we'd done to that delivery guy. But we never told anyone our secret. We promised we would take it to our graves with us.

We had two lakes, a pool, and a small clubhouse in our community. There was a very steep hill near one of those lakes. One day my friends and I decided to tell Lenny to sit on the crossbar of his bike and go down that hill. He agreed, and took off. But he couldn't reach the brakes, so he barreled across the road below and crashed into the woods. He came out all bloodied, and his bike looked like a pretzel. Lenny didn't listen to our suggestions after that.

One day my mom and little brother Alex took a walk to a friend's house on the other side of the lake. When Alex jumped in the lake with his tube, it fell off. He couldn't swim and started screaming. My mom and her friend could not swim either. Thank God my older brother Eddie was riding up with his bike. He heard the commotion, jumped into the lake, and saved poor Alex.

2

PUBERTY

M Y ONLY REGRET WAS THAT CHILDHOOD flew by very fast and I had to start growing up.

I was shocked into the reality of the big cruel world at thirteen. On Halloween night, I was walking with two of my girlfriends on West 11 Street in Brooklyn. A group of about ten boys began to attack us. My friends managed to escape, but I was left there on the ground and was mauled and assaulted. Once they dragged me into an alley, it felt as if there twenty hands all over me at the same time. Though I wasn't actually raped, the incident left me with many emotional scars.

Life contains many complexities of which cruelty to women is one. I never told my mother and father about it, because I knew it would pain them very much to know what had been done to their daughter. I loved them very much and felt that I was old enough to handle the situation myself. I recognized some of the boys too, but, embarrassed and frightened by what had happened to me, I didn't pursue the issue.

If I had it to do over again, I know I would report the incident to the police and maybe saved the humiliation and possible rape of another young girl. Wouldn't it be wonderful if we could undo all the mistakes in our lives.

But this, alas, is not the way it works!

Little Nancy from Brooklyn had quite an interesting childhood. She started kindergarten at PS 97.

Way back in September 1948, I began my schooling. I still remember the little tables and chairs in my kindergarten class. Mrs. Fazio was a wonderful teacher. Though I only went half a day, that class was the basis for a very pleasant educational experience.

How I loved to play and use the finger-paints. All those bright colors smeared on those large pieces of paper hooked onto an easel gave me a very elated feeling. I looked forward to going to school. Even in first grade, when I was placed in Health class, I still looked forward to my five days a week at school.

Why health class? The school officials thought I was too skinny, so that's where I went. The class consisted of five grades combined into one. It was like *Little House on the Prairie*, being in a one-room school house. We had five rows with six students in each row. Our teacher, Mrs. Hoffmen, would teach one row at a time. After lessons, we took out our cots from a large closet: nap time. After that, we ate lunch in the basement lunchroom. They only served soup and peanut butter-and-jelly sandwiches. (So much for peanut allergies.)

Playtime in the schoolyard was lots of fun. We had punch ball and dodge ball, and we ran races. When we returned to our second-floor classroom, snacks were always served, so we would gain some weight and return to regular class assignments.

I stayed there for four years. My older cousin, Lenny, long recovered from his biking catastrophe, was also in the skinny class. I guess being skinny ran in the family.

I'm sure I had a different learning experience from most other kids. Being in a class that included grades one through six was very enlightening, because we had an opportunity to learn from those age differences, and I'm sure kids in one-room schoolhouses all over the country must have learned the same way.

Lenny and I had many happy as well as unhappy experiences together. Each day after school let out, we walked to his house because my mother was taking care of my Aunt Lucy, who was very ill at the time. I can still hear her moaning and crying because she didn't want to die and leave her two young children without a mother. But her fight ended one day when her heart gave out because of the powerful and debilitating cancer medication she was taking.

After her death, Lenny and I became as close as brother and sister because he was always at *my* house. He changed into a very nervous and neurotic person. One day in the schoolyard, we were playing Lead the Blind Man. I closed my eyes and Lenny led me right into a tree. It had a one-foot-high border around it, so when I fell in, my face hit the tree. I fractured my nose and bled all over the place. After that I was very careful about which games I would play with him.

When I was in fourth grade I couldn't understand why two of the boys followed me home from school each day, throwing rocks at me. I had been raised to be nice to other people, so I tried to talk to them, but to no avail.

Finally, one day, one of the two boys was absent and I figured it was then or never. I hit the one following me in the face with my school bag.

They never bothered me again. It was a lesson that has stayed with me to this day. Always try to work things out peaceably, but if you have no choice, if you feel like a rat in a corner, you have to use whatever force you need to protect yourself.

In the fifth grade, I finally left health class and was treated like a normal child. I was just as smart as all the other students, though I'd had much less instruction than they had.

Below my class was the CRMD class. (They no longer have these types of classes. The acronym stood for Children with Retarded Mental Disabilities.)

"No," I yelled at my girlfriend one day in fifth grade. "I don't *believe* it. You must be lying. How could you make up such a terrible story? There *must* be some other way of having a baby."

During my childhood I had not been aware of sex, never wondered how babies were made. I was more interested in the outdoor life—swimming, playing ball, biking, running, mountain climbing, and, most of all, the inconsequential street games such as Johnny on the Pony, Ringalevio, Kick the Can, and just plain jump rope.

At twelve years old, though, I became a woman. My mother told me a little about menstruation. She totally left out, though, the most significant details of the sexual lives of men and women.

In school the subject of sex was taboo. There were no educational classes in which instruction could be provided. Television was in its infancy then, so choices in programs were limited. The only way a child eventually found out about sex was in the streets.

I remember the day my girlfriend Rosalie revealed to me that a man had to stick his thing into a woman's private parts in order to make a baby. I was mortified. I was embarrassed. I had a million thoughts buzzing through my brain at the same time. I answered, "Oh, I would *never* do anything like that," thinking that there *must* be another way to make a baby, and another way for the baby to be born, because I couldn't digest the ways in which my girlfriend had described intercourse and birth.

I feel that sex education in the classroom is a marvelous thing. We have come a long way in preparing our youth for life's realities. I certainly wish *I* had had a better enlightenment. My most embarrassing moment in grammar school was when my sixth-grade teacher asked me if I used deodorant. I bathed at least three times a week, but my parents had never told me about deodorant, I suppose because they were raised in a small, backward town in Sicily and had no inkling of the vast number of products we had access to in America.

When I first began to menstruate, my mother gave me a folded baby diaper to wear. I can still remember the awful feelings I had when I washed the stains away. As I got older, I discovered pads and realized they were a far better and more sanitary way, but I had to buy them on my own.

Growing up in an Italian neighborhood, I didn't have much contact with black people. I never felt any prejudice against them, as I do today. In the eight grade I had a black science teacher. I loved that man. He was the best teacher I had all through my school years. It wasn't until about 1970 that I began to start feeling prejudice against blacks. I don't enjoy having these feelings, but I can't deny their existence.

In seventh grade, I went to Boody Junior High School. In all my school years, Mr. Grant was my favorite teacher. It made no difference to me then that he was black. I didn't see color at that time. But in the mid-1950s, things started to change between the races, and not for the better. High school was a blast. I never had to study and always got good grades. We started a club called the Artells. We threw many parties, including pajama parties—all girls, of course.

3

HIGH SCHOOL

IGH SCHOOL WAS A BREEZE FOR ME. I never studied yet always pulled eighties and nineties. Maybe the fact that I paid attention in school and had extremely good teachers who cared about the students' learning process accounts for those good grades. I always did my assignments and handed them in on time, because I enjoyed getting the grades.

Friends have been an important part of my life. I made many new ones in high school, some of whom I have retained to this day. We partied and went on outings together.

The year is 1958, and I'm fifteen. I'm going to let you have a peek into my diaries, word for word.

January 3

Dear diary, Johnny looked real handsome today. Sometimes I get to thinking, why do I go out with him? But I know better than that. He is just a Romeo and not for me. I haven't seen Rich since that Sunday I went out with him. But I'm beginning to get over him. I think I'm going back to Bob. I sure wish he would write to me or call. My piano teacher was supposed to come over today. I don't know what happened to him. I wrote a letter to Janet today. I hope she writes back. It would be nice to hear from her again.

January 17

Dear diary, I got a letter from Barbara today. She said Carol Rao told her Bob is going to write to me. I hope he doesn't take all year; I want to hear from him. I went roller skating tonight. I had a pretty good time. On the way out I saw Richie. He said hello. I didn't get any kind of feeling seeing him. But now as I'm ready to go to bed, I'm beginning to think how cute he looked. Raymond was in a marine's uniform. He looked real handsome.

February 23

Dear diary, I met this fella Ron at a party last

night. Today I went on a date with him. I think he is a wonderful guy: manners, personality, looks, he has them all. I'm going to start writing to him. He is stationed at the Navy base in New London, Connecticut. When we were getting out of the car at Fran's house, there was all water and snow. Ron carried me to the sidewalk. I don't think I'll ever forget that. I had a wonderful time with a wonderful guy.

March 27

Dear diary, Ron hasn't written me in two days. I'm so worried. All kinds of things are running through my head. Maybe he was in an accident. Maybe he doesn't like me anymore. I don't know what to think. I'm so crazy about him, I'm going nuts. I cried so much tonight, just thinking about it. Every time I hear our song, I want to be in his arms. Why does he have to be so far way? I miss him terribly, Called up Jo today; she said not to worry about Ron. He is probably very busy.

May 31

Dear diary, spent half of my day in the beauty parlor. It looks so nice. I hope Ron likes it. I want to look beautiful for him. With my face, it's pretty hard, though. Tonight I had the most wonderful Sweet Sixteen party any girl could have. There was such a crowd. The one person I needed most at the beginning of the night wasn't there, though. Ron came to the party at eleven o'clock. I was so hurt. But after he explained it, I didn't feel so bad. He gave me a beautiful medal and a little fake dog. I liked them more than all my gifts.

September 23

Dear diary, I played the part of a fresh and sophisticated girl today in dramatics class. I wish I could be a fresh person who didn't care about other people's feelings. But I guess I just can't be like that. Especially with Ron. As much as he hurts me, I could never do it back to him. Went to the Sea Cadets tonight. I always enjoy going there. But I do wish those kids would pay a little more attention.

January 22, 1959

Time keeps flying by so fast. Here it is eleven months that I know Ron. My lover man. I went ice-skating with the girls in the club today. I've never gone before, so I had a pretty rough time— although I didn't fall once. Received a letter from

Ron today. I knew he'd write. In just two weeks he'll be back in the States. Oh, my love, I miss you terribly. Please hurry back to me.

Here is a letter I wrote to Ron during that time but never mailed.

March 26, 1959

Dear Ron,

I constantly think of you, Ron. When I'm in school, doing my work, I'm always daydreaming. Dreaming of being in your arms again. We never have enough time. But someday, God willing, we will always be together. Yes, my darling, and no one will be able to separate us. My love and yearning for you grow stronger with each passing day.

As I go to bed at night, the stars and moon shine in my room, reflecting my radiation. The radiation of the warmth I send off just dreaming of being in your arms. As the sun rises in the morning, I also rise with you in my thoughts. There is not a moment in my life when I don't reminisce about our love. But as much as I need your love, I can be happy in another way. The thing I want most in this world is for you to make something out of yourself. I want you to go to

*college and study and get ahead. Then, someday,
if God spares you, you may come back and ask
for my hand in marriage. Oh, that will be a wonderful day. With the sun shining, bands playing,
people shouting with glee. And you and I will be
on the sidelines, watching all the merrymaking.
Hand in hand, we will walk together in the sun.
Love is an eternal fire, and my flame will forever
burn.*

September 7

*Dear diary, this morning I woke up Ron. He
looked so cute all in white with his golden tan. It
was hard, for today, to be with him. I know I
love him very much. But I also know Johnny is
in my heart too. I cried in front of Ron today because I thought that I might never see him again.
All the times we've spent together, all the kisses
and embraces—I've soul-kissed him quite a few
times this weekend. I really wanted to. After we
said good-bye, I cried so hard on the way home.
Good-bye, my love.*

December 18

*Dear diary, Pete S. and I went to New York
to the show. I had a real swell time. He and I
seem to get along pretty well. But, then again,*

practically every guy I've dated I got along pretty good with on the first few dates. The thing is that the guy always falls for me, and I don't return it. I hope this doesn't happen with Pete. He and I are pretty good friends and I hope to keep it like that. If it is at all possible.

April 26, 1960

Dear diary, I was so happy tonight when Petey asked me to go steady that I just could have died from joy. It took him so long to get up enough nerve. He was so cute in the different ways that he was trying to tell me. I hope that I'll always remain as happy as I am tonight. I hope that Ron doesn't bother my thoughts and just leaves me alone. I'm trying so hard to fight him off. I hope I can really do it.

May 3

Dear diary, Oh, God, I don't know what to do. I just want to die. I keep saying it will never happen again, but it always does. I just can't keep Pete's hands off me. I don't know if it is love or just some attraction for sex. I need someone's help, but I don't know where to go. I go to confession every week and I ask for forgiveness from God, but then I go ahead and commit the sin all over again. How can I be good—it is so hard!

4

MARRIAGE AND CHILDREN

HAVING BEEN RAISED IN THE ATMOSPHERE of a so-called perfect nuclear family—mother, father, three children, house in the city, summer home, a car and an upper middle-class income—I felt that my life's purpose was to marry and have a happy little family of my own. On May 4, 1963, Peter and I were married. Here are some of my diary entries, and a letter I wrote to him, from this time.

May 4, 1963

The sun was shining so brightly on this Saturday in May. The temperature outside was in the 90s, and my temperature was pretty high, too. It was the day of my wedding. I was going to marry the true love of my life. Pete and I had been dating for three and a half years. The fun and laughs were only a small part of the wonderful times we had together.

The church ceremony was beautiful. Pledging my love and devotion for all the years of my life was such an easy thing to do. Our parents were proud and happy to see us getting married. Rose and Joseph Sabatino and Frances and Alexander Saparata had tears throughout the entire ceremony.

My maid of honor was my cousin Providence Stefanko, and Pete's best man was Anthony Sabatino. The bridal party consisted of family and friends. Eddie Saparata and his wife Frances were attendants, along with Alexander Saparata, John Kelly, Al Grancagnolo, Connie Spitale, Barbara Maffai, and Joann Lo Bianco. The pillow boy and flower girl were Lenny and Kathy Pirrello.

It seemed like the night went on forever, with lots of dancing, laughing, eating, and drinking. The wedding reception finally ended, and off we went to the hotel. My beautiful white negligee was on for only a little while. The rest of the evening I will not talk about because it is private. In those days, the consummation of the marriage *took place on the wedding night. It was a beautiful time for Pete and me. The lovemaking was hot and heavy. After those years of waiting, the rapture came out at the International Hotel at Idlewild Airport in Brooklyn, New York.*

My letter to Pete follows:

May 5, 1963
Dear Pete,

The memories of last night I will always treasure. They say it only hurts for a little while and I guess the refrain is right.

I am so very happy. I know that our life together will be filled with much happiness. As long as we both try to give and not take, I'm sure our life will be one worth living. Then when the children come we mustn't forget each other. Don't ever let other people put obstacles in our way. Let's always try to work out our own problems. I hope I will always love you as much as I do this moment.

Your wife,
Nancy

We traveled to Europe on our honeymoon and visited our parents' birthplace in Sicily.

What a magnificent little island Sicily is. It has beautiful stone towns set high up in the rocky hills. We were told that some of the towns had been built around the time of Christ. In those days, stone was the main weapon material for protection against one's enemies, so towns were built on the highest mountains, so people could throw stones down at anyone trying to attack.

It was in Italy that I learned to appreciate my Italian heritage. I learned to enjoy demitasse coffee and wine during my one-month stay there. We filled our one-liter bottles of wine at the wineries for twenty cents a bottle. The groceries had plenty of bread, salami, and cheese, so we enjoyed many picnics in the open air. Some of our Sicilian relatives led very difficult lives trying to survive in those antiquated surroundings. I can remember how sorry I felt for them; I left half of my belongings there. They wouldn't let us buy any food for them, so we had to eat whatever was put on the table.

One day they killed a chicken and I had to pluck all the feathers out myself. We had a feast that night, because meat was on the table. My aunt Maria thought that it was a treat to give me a glass of warm goat's milk, too. I couldn't hurt her feeling, so I drank it with much hidden revulsion.

Italian families tend to have many petty jealousies,

which inadvertently produce small family feuds. The behavior has been carried over to Italian communities here in the United States as well.

PETE AND I TRIED TO START A FAMILY for about six years. With much frustration and disappointment, we finally decided that, if we were going to have children, we would have to adopt them.

In those days it was difficult for some Italians to accept the fact that there would be no natural offspring. Even more upsetting was the fact that the husband would not be able to pass on the family name to his sons. I can still hear my father-in-law's voice insisting that he wanted a child from his own blood. That remark cut right through me like a sword.

But when the twins came along, his attitude couldn't have been any more loving than if they had been from his own blood line.

I was taught to keep a clean house, cook nourishing meals, take good care of the children, and above all always keep my husband happy. This is exactly what I've been trying to do for my entire married life. There have been pitfalls, obstacles in my path, but for the most part I consider myself a very lucky woman.

I love my husband and three sons very much. I also have a life of my own, even though I don't work outside of the home. My outside activities give me a chance to just be me. This I feel my mother, and her mother before her, were never able to do. They lived very straight-and-narrow lives and were never able to branch out into the real world.

I wish my mother was still here today, but God decided that he needed her more than her family did. She was so very special and precious to me, and, though many years have gone by since her death, the pain of the loss is still with me. I have many moments to this day when I can sit and cry.

We had a very different relationship than the usual mother- and-daughter one. My mom was a simple woman with a tremendous heart. Everyone who knew her came to love her. At her funeral, many people I had never met came who told me what a wonderful person my mother was.

She always made me laugh. It's very important to be able to laugh at insignificant things. I lost that ability after her death and have only regained it over the past three or four years.

My husband has stood by my side through all the bad times as well as the good. I love him very much for always being there for me when I needed him. Life is about caring and loving, and I know I've had my fair share of both.

My three sons mean the world to me, and I've tried very hard to show them the proper roads to travel on. When the twins were in college, I was very proud of both of them, because they had a respect for life and a need for education.

Here are an array of diary entries about my boys, from when the first two came to us to when they were long grown.

June 13, 1969

Today was one of the happiest days of my life. Pete and I went to the adoption agency to pick up our two-and-a-half-month-old twin boys. Our first glimpse of them was one of sheer happiness and delight at how beautiful and alike they looked.

Alice was waiting in the lobby when we came down. She had tears in her eyes when she saw them.

The trip home was anxious—to have them for our own, and to have them be well. We stopped at the shop to let Pop see them. He was very happy. When we got to 11th Street, my mother started crying when she realized there were two of them. My mother-in-law came outside with her crutches.

We decided to name them after their grandfathers, Joseph and Alexander. It was splendid seeing everyone so surprised and happy, but most of all there was the happiness Pete and I felt at fi-

nally becoming parents.

The twins were bald, with light skin and blue eyes, and big hands and feet. We figure they'd grow to over six feet. We put them both in one crib because that's all we had at the time. How cute they looked. Saint Anthony's day was a real blessing for us this year. We gave both boys the middle names of Anthony.

June 26

We moved to Staten Island today. It was a beautiful day for Pete and me to be moving to our new home. My mother came to stay with us a few days to help out. Alice and Cookie worked their fingers to the bone helping us clean up. Even Maria helped out. Two days later, they brought the twins out to us. Aunt Tina had watched Joseph, and Fran had watched Alex. I was overjoyed to see them. I had missed them so much, even though we had only gotten them the week before.

Ernie loaned us his crib, so we were able to separate them.

August

In August they started turning over. We kept them in one playpen. They were very healthy and good babies, always kicking and laughing.

We had the boys blessed at Saint Patrick's in Staten Island. Anthony and Jeanie are Joseph's godparents, and Provie and Alex are Alexander's. Later that day, we had a big party for them. Just the thought of those two little monkeys being our sons brought us great happiness.

October

Aha, a tooth has finally appeared. Crawling around like two little puppies, and standing up, and now the teeth. Who could ask God for more?

November

Two front teeth apiece.

December

Six teeth in each mouth. They look so cute with all those little pearls. They both say, "Da-Da," but I doubt if they know what that means yet. Joey sat up first, and now Alex is right there with him. This month was the first time we had them sick. Joey had a red throat, and Al red ears.

January 1970

We hope this will be a good year with peace everywhere. I'd like for Alex and Joey to grow up in a safe world. Both boys are now saying "Da-Da" and "Ma-Ma," and I think they're beginning to understand the meaning of these words. Alex has learned to clap his hands. Joey seems a little bit lazy; I think it will take him longer. Alex has always been more of a bully to Joey. If I put them together, Joey always ends up on the bottom, crying, because Alex is hitting and pulling his hair. (They finally got rid of that Yul Brenner look.)

February 4

The twins are the funniest thing to watch. I just caught them touching each other's heads and laughing hysterically. They have such fun with the silliest things. They also seem to be able to understand when we tell them not to touch something. They both walk all around their cribs and playpens, but neither has let go yet.

February 5

Joey had his first fall today. He stood up in his highchair and fell over. He cried quite a bit, but thank God he is all right.

February 6

The twins went to their first birthday party today. It was for Doreen, who is seven years old. They had such a good time with all the other children. They love to play with other little kids.

February 8

Alex got his seventh tooth today (a bottom one). Joey has been getting a little daring today— as far as letting go when he is standing up. No signs they want to walk yet.

March 7

Both my little guys have colds and coughs. No fever, though. This is the second time they've been sick since we have them. They are so good, though, even when they are discomforted.

March 13

Joey is eighteen and a half pounds, thirty-one inches long; Alex is nineteen pounds, thirty-one inches long. They're starting to walk now by holding onto something. Won't be long before they are on their own.

March 28

The little fellas had their first birthday party today. They looked so smart in their blue-striped vests and blue bowties. Everyone gave them beautiful gifts.

April 30

Joey took his first steps alone tonight. My mother, Pete, and I were in the kitchen. We were all thrilled to see that little guy walk.

May 1

Smallpox vaccinations. Joey got it in the right arm, Alex in the left. Both about twenty and a half pounds and thirty-one inches long.

Alex took his first steps at the Maffai house on 8th Street. The little fella gave Pete and me such a thrill.

May 18

I have them both getting their first haircuts.

June 13, 1970

This day last year, we were on top of the world when we came home with our two little dolls. Alex is now walking on his own but still a little insecure. He throws his left foot when walking. He may need a corrective shoe. Joey is walking around like he knows it all. He is such a silly little guy.

I noticed today that Alex had gotten his first molar on the right side.

July 4

The twins have all four molars cutting through. They have, I must say, been pretty casual about it all. We took them to Provie and George's for three days. They behaved beautifully, and I think they had a nice time.

August

Alex got a cold in his ear, and Joey in his throat. Seems like they are prone to the same illnesses. They both have twelve teeth.

September

Alex and Joey have come a long way in one year's time, they both have quite a vocabulary:

> *Mommy*
> *Daddy*
> *Hi, Daddy*
> *Nanni*
> *Pappi*
> *Granpapa (Joey)*
> *go away (Joey)*
> *what (Joey)*
> *boo boo here (Alex)*

car

doggie

baby

good

no

nose

eyes

shoe

out

draw

door

hot

sit down

ball

thank you

beer

bread

November

The little guys are now nineteen and a half months old. They go up the stairs, and I am teaching them how to come down. They can eat some table food by themselves, but I prefer to feed them. Their vocabulary is steadily growing. We feel that they are very bright children. Alex still seems tougher than Joey. But in some ways he is very sensitive.

December 22

Today was the twins' first experience seeing snow. They were very excited and just looked out the window in amazement. They can now use three or four words to make sentences. They can count to three. Alex doesn't need corrective shoes any longer. One day Alex seems like the tougher one, and the next day it's the reverse. They do what I would call a normal amount of fighting. They have loved music from a very early age as well and enjoy dancing to it.

December 25, 1970

We spend Christmas as usual at my Mom and Dad's house. The twins were very frightened when Santa Claus came in. I think the noise and excitement from everyone got them more scared. My brother Al was Santa this year, and I guess he was enough to scare anyone. But the boys really enjoyed opening their gifts.

March 3, 1971

Alex still weighs a few more ounces than Joey. They are twenty-five pounds. They speak four-word sentences now. They wear a size three and count to three.

March 9

The twins now eat at the dinner table with us. I suppose that's normal for almost two. Joey sings the rainy day song. Alex is always coming over to kiss me. He is the more affectionate and sensitive of the two, although at times he seems so tough. Alex puts on the TV while Joey sits and watches from his chair. He also adjusts the antenna. Then Joey opens the little door and adjusts his volume control.

March 15

Both boys are now saying, "I love you." Joey says everything like a parrot. Alex, I have to prod a little.

We took the twins to Fran today. I felt really terrible leaving them.

April 25

Landed at Kennedy at midnight on Sunday. Had a marvelous time in Italy, but missed my little guys something awful.

Joey had chicken pox while staying at Fran's, and Alex got them this week.

May 2

Jeanie said Anthony and she had a great time

with them, but then again, who wouldn't? They are now thirty-five inches tall, having grown another inch.

July

We took the boys to Pennsylvania for a week. The two fish loved playing in three feet of water. They had no fear at all.

October 6

Alexander is now doing a lot of talking. He is trained as far as wetting but not number two. His temper is getting stronger now.

Joey is just about all trained now. He loves to talk on the phone, and he rides his bike well.

They both eat everything Pete and I eat. They give us so much happiness that it's hard to re-member what life was without them.

January 1972

Time seems to fly by. Christmas was lots of laughs with the boys. Alex was so afraid of Santa. I hope he grows out of it by next year. Joey was a little frightened, but then he went over to him. Philie was Santa this year. He looked just fabulous. The only one missing was my brother Al. It was the first Christmas with-

out him. I hope he comes home soon. I had
the flu over New Years, and so did the twins.
It breaks my heart to see those little tots so
sick.

They are so funny when they play alone.
They carry on a conversation like two old men.
I think Joey is giving the orders now.

March 28, 1972

My babies turned three today. The time just
passes by too fast to suit me. They are developing
beautifully.

August 1972

We all had a wonderful summer. We took
the twins to Host Farm. They are just like two
fish. No fear of water. They ate beautifully in
the restaurant. I don't mind taking them any-
where.

September 1972

Uncle Tom Saparata passed away this month.
I'll never forget how much he loved the twins and
played with them. I'll miss that man. First my
grandmother, now Uncle Tom; I suppose, as you
grow older and your kids start getting big, the
older folks dwindle away.

Christmas 1972

Christmas is always the happiest time of the year for me. The little guys got so many gifts from everyone. They weren't afraid of Santa Claus this year. We had Philie dress up again.

Their vocabulary is ever-increasing. I wonder why they remain so skinny—after all, they do eat just as much as other kids.

March 28, 1973

Four years old. The twins had their first birthday party with friends. They were so excited that Peter, Anthony, Nickie, Tricia, Joseph, and Ritchie were coming. We had a pizza pie for a cake.

They played musical chairs and Pin-the-Tail.

April 1973

We had my dad's retirement surprise party on April 7. It was really wonderful. The biggest surprise for him was when Alex walked in. He flew in from Canada.

May

Pete and I had our tenth anniversary. I hope the love we now share will always grow. Joey and Alex have brought a deeper meaning to our lives.

My mom had her sixtieth birthday party. Dad had roses delivered. She was like a little child when she saw them.

Summer 1973

Joey and Alex have such a large capacity for love. Their personalities are forming beautifully. They don't seem to have any meanness in them. Of course, I have to deal with the usual fighting with each other, but five minutes later it's all over with. At four years old, they're still like two fish. They must have excellent lungs to stay under the water as long as they do. I really believe, if we had a large pool, they would be swimming this year.

August

The boys are now swimming with just those plastic jackets. They really don't hold them up, but their little arms and legs really move around.

Pete and I went on a marriage encounter weekend. It was the most beautiful weekend that I've ever spent with my husband. It really gives you the ability to take off your masks and learn how to love one another. I'm filled with so much love and peace with myself and God. I've never felt this close to God before. Instead of looking at the world as a horrible place, this weekend enabled me to take off my dark glasses and look at all the beauty around us. I hope the feeling of love will rub off on the twins. They already have so much love as children; maybe now they will be able to retain it.

December 1974

Christmas was beautiful this year. It was the first holiday we spent at home. We had both our families over. Doug Slymen played Santa Claus. It is so funny and wonderful to see the twins still believing in Santa. I wonder if it will be their last year.

April 1975

We went down to Miami and then to Disney World. It was a beautiful vacation. The boys were kinda restless in the car. But I suppose that's natural for six-year-olds. My brother Al spent most of the time with us.

Summer of 1975

The twins know how to swim and dive. They

are totally on their own—even in ten feet of water.

Baseball is their favorite sport. Joey has a beautiful batting arm. They both ride a two-wheeler very well. I suppose my little boys are growing. I still can't believe they're six years old.

August 25, 1975

Well, here we are again: Today we brought home little Michael. He is such a honey. Is it possible for two people to have so much happiness in just one life? He has reddish blond hair and blue eyes with light skin. We totally shocked everyone. The flowers and champagne were like a wedding. Michael was really welcomed. The twins have already held and fed him. They took to the idea immediately.

We didn't have to buy a thing for Michael. All our friends and neighbors came through with all the equipment.

September 1975

Joey and Alex have started losing teeth and entered the first grade. It's hard to grasp that my little twinnies are really growing up. It seems much easier now that I'm home alone with Michael, though. I have all day to love him up.

October

Mom and Pop Sabatino returned from Italy. This has been their first look at the baby. They immediately took to the little tyke.

The baptism was splendid, with Father Arnold presiding and Eddie and Fran as godparents. We then took everyone out to dinner. It was a beautiful and happy day for all of us.

November

Thanksgiving this year was more meaningful than ever to me. I now have three beautiful sons to be proud of. Connie had baby Mark there. With only a two-month difference in their ages, he seems so much bigger than Mike.

December

Brother Al finally got to see Michael. I wish he lived here instead of Miami, but I guess one cannot always have what they want out of life.

The twins still believe in Santa Claus. In all the years that we've had someone dress as Santa, this was the first for Zini. Michael slept through the whole thing.

Sometimes I get a little depressed thinking of how tied up I got myself. But then I realize how much I really wanted another child. At four months Michael has gotten his first tooth.

March 1976

Joey and Alex are seven years old. Where did the time go? They are reading. Joey seems to grasp the words a little faster.

April 1980

Here it is four years later, and I'm happy as a lark. Michael is such a smart, beautiful child. I call him "the professor." He does everything so quickly. When he first started talking before he was a year old, he used adult words. He is only four now, but very mature for his age.

Joey always remained a little ahead of Alex in reading. The two of them have come such a long way. They were the cutest things when they joined Little League. They love baseball. For that matter they love all sports. They have been on two swimming teams and seem to do very well.

Pop died three years ago this July. We all took it very badly. Michael was only two years old, but he still remembers his grampa. He kept waiting for him to come back.

Uncle Sal also passed away last month. I sup-

pose now that I'm older I'll see a lot more of my family leaving us. The new come in, and the old go out.

Uncle Pete is very sick and will have to go on the dialysis machine three times a week.

Gramma Pirrello is in the hospital and will soon go into a nursing home. She is almost ninety-one and hard to handle.

June 9, 1981

My life was shattered today by the passing away of my beautiful mother. She had open-heart surgery and went two weeks later, having developed sepsis, which they could not cure. She was on a respirator for two weeks, so she could not talk. I have such an ache inside me that almost seems unbearable. I know the weeks and months ahead will be empty without her, and I simply cannot believe I'll never see her again. I loved her so very much. But I have my wonderful husband and my beautiful boys to help me through the months ahead.

July 1981

We had a small birthday party for my father but my heart wasn't in it. Doreen graduated. I felt like a mummy at her ceremony.

Angela had a year-old birthday party. I just couldn't cope too well with anything.

Even Michael's birthday in August wasn't too happy for me. I suppose it's going to take a long time.

May 30, 1987

We had a wonderful graduation party for Joey and Alex. How fast the time has gone. Eighteen years ago, we brought home two beautiful little bundles of blue. Now they've graduated from St. Joseph by the Sea High School.

All the family and friends came to the party. It was gratifying to see them. I really enjoyed dancing with my sons. I suppose the next time will be on their wedding days.

July 25

Dad is eighty years old. Oh, how I wish my mom could have been at the great party we threw for him. He was very happy. Alex came in from Miami with Debbie and Allison. Eddie, Fran, and the kids looked great. Paul Patane wrote him a fantastic scroll. He enjoyed the band very much because it was his kind of music. I hope he lives to a hundred, nice and healthy.

July 4

We all had a grand old time at the Impasta-tos. It was nice to get together with everyone for the Fourth. It's been about four or five years since we went up there for the picnic.

July 5

When we came home, the boys went to the club. They came home around 8:30, and Michael went across to Anthony's house where he pro-ceeded to blow himself up with fireworks. His leg and hand were very badly burned.

He was in excruciating pain for over a month. He also will need a skin graft on a large area of his leg. If I could trade places with him, I would, just to alleviate the pain that he suffered.

July 17

Michael is having the skin graft done today. After two weeks of pain and suffering, he's going to get a little bit of relief. He was in dreadful pain this morning when I had to give him a shower. His leg was shaking badly, and I know he is ter-ribly scared about being operated on.

July 24

Michael has come home from the hospital.

He is weak and looks pale, but thank God I know he will be well soon.

Later

Today he is all recovered except for the scarring on his right thigh. I now realize that God was good to him by sparing him further damage to his body. We can only guide our children to the right paths; we cannot always be there to make sure that they are not straying from them. Children need to explore and have a certain amount of freedom, and sometimes these tragic things can happen. I feel that I grew up with a sense of freedom and wonder, and this is what I've tried to share with my children—but there will always be a down side.

August 23

Happy Birthday, Pete and Michael. We all had a delightful, sunny day on the deck. My mother-in-law really enjoyed herself out there till almost six o'clock. So the little boy is now twelve years old. How the time does fly. I'm happy that his leg is coming along just fine.

September 7

Our last day at the swim club. It was really

nice to see all the big guys together there. I sure hope next year will be a good one for all of us.

May 4, 1988

Here I am twenty-five years with the same wonderful man. I still love him very much and hope we live out the next twenty-five together. We have gone through so many things together, good and bad, and we made it through. I love our children so much. They've always made me very proud of them. It's hard to believe that Joey and Alex are finished with their first year of college. Michael has had a terrible year physically and I hope it doesn't leave mental scars in him.

May 19, 1988

It was great having a birthday party for my brother, Alex. We had a nice crowd for dinner and then a few of his old friends came over afterwards. I love cooking and having parties. I just wish I didn't get so tired. Thank God I still have my dad to help me out. He does a great job with all the vegetables and fruits.

I hope to get to see a lot of my brother while he's home. I've really missed him.

December 1988

It was wonderful to see everyone's happy faces this Christmas. Lil' Anthony was our new edition to the family this year. It's so very fine to see life go on and realize how happy two people can be with a new baby. We made Zini play Santa Claus again. I think this was the last time to use him. Joe and Al have bought a Ford Bronco truck. I like to see them have everything good. I only want the best for all my sons.

March 4, 1980

Oh, what an exciting day it was today to see my brother Alex finally get married! Everything was perfect. The ceremony was brief, but everyone who really cared was at the church. If only my mother had been there. I knew she must have been watching from heaven, because she had always wanted this day to come. My boys looked so handsome all dressed up. I'm so proud of the three of them, because they do the best they can. Michael could do more!

1983

My mother-in-law had a brain abscess. She lived in the Eger nursing home for ten years.

April 1989

The boys went away again. I worry so much when they are on Spring Break. Even though Alex went to West Palm Beach with Lou, I still worried just as much. The twins are all grown up. I've seen them through potty training to college. I think the potty training was a lot easier than listening to their complaints and moodiness at twenty years of age.

May 1989

The whole family went on an outstanding vacation to Disney. It was the best we've ever had together. We stayed at the nicest hotel. It's funny, really, but I'm remembering the Disney vacation we took in 1980. That was also in May, two years after my mom's death. Going away with Pete and all my sons made me feel good for the first time in two weeks. Now, at the Grand Floridian, I really had the time of my life. Everything was clean and beautiful.

June 1989

Our baby Mike graduated from IS 24. It was exciting to see him in his cap and gown. In September he will go to St. Joseph by the Sea High School. I hope he does well and will be happy there. He's getting to be such a handsome young man.

July 29, 1989

Li'l Alex was born. I wish my mother was here to see him.

August

Dad, Joe, Mike and I went to Florida to see baby Al. I felt as if I was the grandmother. He is so adorable.

September 1989

I was very hurt for Mike, because he didn't make the baseball team at school. His brothers played for Sea, and I know he must have been very disappointed.

December 1989

Brother Al and his family came up for Christmas. Everything was perfect, except for Mom not being there. I loved babysitting for Al. He is the cutest little and happiest baby I've seen in a while. I wish they lived closer.

1990

Mike hasn't made any teams at Sea. I guess

everyone is different. I thought he always had the potential to be a great athlete. I don't think he gives his all.

September 1991

We just finished on the hottest summers I can remember. It started in May in the 90s and it still is going strong.

I'm so happy we finally added a pool to our backyard. I just love to swim.

Joe and Al have graduated college with accounting degrees. I am enormously proud of them. When they marched up to the podium to receive their diplomas, my heart was pounding, and I couldn't stop sweating. We all went to Castle Harbor Restaurant for a food orgy. Later in September, we had a large celebration for the twins at the Holiday Inn. It turned out excellently. Pete and I are utterly proud to have those guys as our children.

My brother Alex and baby Al came for the party. Li'l Al is so cute.

December 1991

Christmas was wonderful, having us all together. When Alex comes from Florida and everyone is together, I seem to miss my mother even more. Last June, it was ten years since she died. It seems unbelievable that my precious mother wasn't here to see all the fine occasions the family has celebrated.

May 1992

Provie gave a dinner party at her house for my fiftieth birthday. It was the best present I could have gotten, just to be with the cousins that I had had so very much fun with growing up. Pete and I have also grown up together, in another sense. I love being with him in every sense of the word. I know my life wouldn't be complete if he wasn't at my side. I thank God for all the inspiring times we've been able to share together: my Big Boy Pete.

June 1992

We made a small deck around the pool. The backyard looks beautiful. I love being back there. I just wish the weather holds up so I can get my swimming exercise in every day!

September 1992

The summer was pleasant but not hot. Great sleeping weather but not good for swimming or the beach. I felt bad for Joe and Al, because they rented a room at the Jersey shore and almost every weekend was terrible.

Mike had to go to summer school again. I guess he doesn't seem to mind because he doesn't complain about it at all. He really disappointed me about Driver's Ed. We paid for the course and he just went there two times. He said the kids were younger than him and was embarrassed to tell me.

5

MOVING ON

SOMETIMES WHEN I'M ALL ALONE and quiet, I can re-flect on my past and think of all the fun times I had. I remember my grandfather, my father, and my uncle Tom making wine every year. My father had a sub-cellar underneath the regular basement. This room had no windows except for an air shaft that went up into the backyard. The smell of the fresh grapes being crushed by the press will forever remain in my mind. It was so delightful to come downstairs on a Saturday morning and see all the work going on. The room contained about ten large wooden barrels. When the wine was all consumed and the barrels had to be cleaned, my father had to chop all the sediment from the bottom. To dry them, a stick of sulfur was placed inside. This method of drying up all the moisture also killed any insects.

Our dinner table always had a bottle of wine on it, along with the most delicious foods my mom prepared. Mother worked only in the home, as I have said, so she had plenty of time to prepare the meals. We always had a first and second dish, then fruit, nuts, black coffee, and dessert. People always dropped by when it was time for the coffee, so Mom made an extra pot. I can still hear the heavy pounding of grandmother's feet coming up the kitchen stairway.

As soon as she sat down, the arguments in Italian erupted. Grandmother owned a house three doors away from us and always had some new problem. Either she was fighting with her neighbors or with her tenants. It was always up to my parents to calm her down. During all that talk, some very funny things were said, and everyone would end up laughing.

The parties that we had for communions, confirmations, graduations, and such always had some ethnic music being played. The tarantella was a joy to dance. We also had bowls of favas to eat. You had to remove the skin from the bean before you could pop it in your mouth. After everyone ate plenty of the beans, the aroma in the room sometimes got a little unpleasant.

Italian pastries were always a plus at these parties, and on the holidays, too. My mother made one pastry in the shape of an apple turnover. It was stuffed with ricotta cheese and bits of chocolate, and fried in oil. We ate them cool with powdered sugar on top. Boy, oh boy, what a delicious taste those *casathedas* had.

My neighborhood was mostly Italian. They were born in different provinces of Italy, which accounted for the many dialects of Italian that were spoken. It is *very* difficult for a Sicilian, say, to understand a person born in Calabria or Bari, but we all seemed to manage very well.

As the seasons progressed, there was always another saint's day to celebrate. Usually the social clubs marched through the streets carrying a large statue of a saint. People pinned money to the ribbons around it. Some of the feasts had bazaars at which you could play games and buy Italian dishes like sausage and peppers, zeppoli, pizza, calzones, clams on the half shell, and so on. There was always something going on in my neighborhood, which made for a very happy childhood when I was younger: I always had something to do.

Sometimes my father took the family to a Chinese restaurant, which was the only other ethnic food that I ate as a child. I now feel that I was raised in a more-or-less closed environment. I can't say whether it was bad or good to have grown up this way, only that I always seemed to enjoy myself. I've lived a happy, fulfilling, and largely blameless life. Why, in nearly eighty years I have had only one run-in with The Law.

I was furious as the police officer wrote up a summons for me for passing a red light. I know I was wrong, because the red light was there. Logically, it should not have been, because it served no safety purpose.

The incident also occurred early in the morning, with no other cars present. I made a left turn against the light. The next thing I heard was the blaring of a police siren behind my car. I was ordered over a loudspeaker to pull over.

In a pleasant voice I explained to the officer that I didn't think the light should be operating on that corner, since it served no logical purpose.

He told me that I had no right to make that judgment.

I told him I would see him in the court and let the judge decide who was right.

I felt a tremendous amount of anger towards the police department, and I was determined to get some sort of sweet revenge. I felt that, if I was able to win the case, the anger that was festering inside me would subside.

The incident had taken place on Arthur Kill Road, where a sewer construction project was under way at the intersection of Tanglewood Road. Arthur Kill Road was blocked off to oncoming traffic by a six-foot wall of dirt. I was only able to make a left turn. The cars driving on Tanglewood could only make a right turn onto Arthur Kill. It would have been impossible for an accident to occur if the traffic department had temporarily shut off the light.

I went back to that corner with a Polaroid camera and took pictures of at least ten different cars going through that same red light. I also drew a map and explained where the police car had been hiding.

At my court appearance, I told the judge that I felt the police department was unjustly ticketing people. The situation was a set-up to trap the drivers. The judge agreed with me, and my case was dropped. As I walked out of the courtroom, I felt a terrific sense of satisfaction. The anger I had once felt no longer existed.

HERE ARE SOME MORE ENTRIES from my diaries that capture the ups and downs, the brightnesses and sorrows, of these passing years.

I have written them down the way I wanted to—not every day and not always in strict chronological sequence. I've skipped many important parts of my life because I'm often writing about events three or four years after the fact. Sometimes I can't remember what I ate last night, let alone remember little incidents years past. I'm trying to do the best I can, so, my dear children, when you read these scattered, fugitive pages, if I have left anything out, please forgive me—-I'm only human. I've tried to give the best I had to you because I love you all, and you deserve the best life has to offer.

April 1989

I'm thinking of all the teasing my younger brother Alex endured as we were growing up. In one instance, I was hiding behind a door down in the basement of the house. As he opened it, I jumped out, and he got so scared that he fell to the floor and started shaking terribly.

Another time, I was sitting on the toilet in the downstairs bathroom when he opened the door. I yelled so loud he started to shake then, too.

I also made potions for him to drink. Thank God I never poisoned him. Kids will be kids.

November 1992

I gave my cousins Provie and Lenny a fiftieth-birthday dinner at my house. We had a very moving time. I prepared all the food, and I hired Marie to clean and serve for the night. It was the first time I hired someone to help me out, and I suppose it won't be the last. Pete played all the right music, so we danced the night away. The next day we had a brunch and continued the party.

Christmas 1992

Everything was great, except brother Al didn't come from Florida. The boys are crazy about him, and we all have a great time when he comes to visit. Richie is having a terrible time with his store. I hope he can sell it and maybe get a normal job. Doreen's new baby Rachel is so pretty, she looks like a fake doll. I can't wait until I become a grandmother. I pray I have nice daughters-in-law, and that my sons find happiness.

New Year's Eve

We celebrated the holiday at Marge and Tom's. We've been such good friends for over twenty years. I was very happy to have my whole family with me, including my father. He was dancing with Margie's sister-in-law Lois and seemed to be having a bang-up time. I know that, one of these days, he won't be with us anymore, so I try to enjoy all the time I have left with him. I still miss my mother, eleven years later.

January 29, 1993

Brother Al and baby Al came to visit this weekend. He is such a beautiful baby. He wasn't feeling well, but he was still a lot of fun. I only wish that they lived closer to us. I remember all the fun times at my mother's house when we had my aunts and uncles nearby. We had a large

*party Saturday night with about thirty people:
lots of food, drink, music, laughs, and talking. I
hired Maria again. I guess I must be getting old,
because I know I need help.*

June 1993

*Mike finally graduated—of course with the
stipulation that he write a report of a religion subject. It has been a grueling four years, and I'm
glad it's over. I can't wait till he starts cooking
school and I hope he finally finds a school he
likes.*

*We had a party for him in the house. It was
loads of fun. Thank God for Maria helping out—
I get very tired lately, and it sure worth it to have
some help. The kids and Pete are also a great
help. I couldn't do it without my wonderful
family.*

June

*I also graduated from C.S.I. this year with an
A.A. degree in Liberal Arts.*

*It sure took me long enough, but I finally
feel I have accomplished something. Barbara
and I have been good friends for so long, and we
graduated college together. We had a great party
with our closest friends and plenty of laughter*

for the graduates. It was marvelous having our long-time friend Joann and her family over—all the grown children to help two old ladies cele-brate!

July 20, 1993

My mother-in-law died today. Though it's been ten years since she's been in Eger, and she has always wanted to die and be with her hus-band, it's still hard to say good-bye. I will miss all the Sunday visits. Somehow, while there were days I would have rather done something else, it was nice having Gramma and the kids around the dinner table. I know I will miss having another woman to talk to. It's hard to say good-bye to another mom.

September 1993

My baby Mike, who wants to become a chef, is going to the New York Restaurant School in Manhattan. It's not as good a school as CIA, but at least he's going somewhere. He didn't study for the entrance exam for CIA, so he failed the math section. I'm sure that he will make a good chef; he's always helping me in the kitchen. Two accountants and one chef: My three fine sons—I love them dearly.

September 1993

Aunt Frances died suddenly. Her heart finally gave out. My father called me from her apartment, and I made it there in fifteen minutes from Staten Island. He was very upset to see his baby sister dead. I suppose all the years of anorexia finally took a toll on her. I tried for years to get her to see a psychologist, but she just yelled at me and said she was fine. I loved my aunt very much, and I know I'll miss her.

Aunt Frances left a will dividing everything equally among her nieces and nephews, and twenty percent to her sister. My father received nothing.

April 1994

The family is dwindling. My Aunt Antoinette passed away just before her ninety-second birthday. I loved both of my father's sisters very much. Each was special to me, and now they are gone. It's very lonely to have no one older to confide in. Sometimes I miss my mother much, much more than at other times.

Because of the death of my aunts, the family has broken apart. My cousins Phil and Phyllis no longer wanted a relationship with us: A stupid misunderstanding over Aunt Frances's will, and a whole family is no longer together. I miss my cousin Cookie an awful lot. We shared our whole lives like sisters. The laughs we had! I shall always try to remember the good times we shared and the love we knew was there for each other.

September 1994

My dad was hit by an out-of-control car while he was shopping for vegetables in Brooklyn. He was pretty well banged up and had a fractured knee. He spent three weeks in Staten Island Hospital and four months in the Eger Nursing Home. It's absolutely amazing that this man survives such strange calamities. This was the third time in his life that he could have died. But it is not his time yet.

Joey is doing very well as an accountant. He has such splendid stamina for studying. He is studying for his CPA exam. I have no doubt in my mind that he will pass.

Alex has remained in the recycling field. The money is good, and I'm sure he likes being his own boss.

Joey has been going out with Kathy for quite a few years now. She is a nice kid, but a little overpowering. I know she's not a very happy person because she has been living alone since her parents divorced. I hope she can find happiness in her life someday.

Alex has been dating Tina for a couple of years now, too. She seems like a very bubbly, happy person. I don't know if Alex truly loves her. I always think he still has Gloria on his mind.

January 1993

Dad came back to my house after being released from Eger. He has made a remarkable recovery. He wants to stay here a couple of months before returning to Brooklyn. I worry about him being alone, but he remains a very independent person. At eighty-seven, he still wants to drive his car. He calls the car "Destry." He even wants to consider buying a new one.

Alex has been living in Pittsburg for a while now. He has matured into a wonderful man since he has been away. I miss him very much. He was always the one to come into my room and chat. I've found it easier to talk with Al than with Joe. Sometimes I feel Joey takes things the wrong way and gets angry. Mike and I can usually talk anytime. I still miss not having a daughter to talk to, though; it's hard to relate to a houseful of men.

July 1995

How sweet it is to have these lobster parties. I made my dad collect about $1,300.00 from an AAA insurance policy. It was found money, so we decided to have a family lobster party for his birthday. He is now eighty-eight years young. Even my brother Al and his family came from Florida for the festivities. I think Sal can win the prize for eating the most lobsters. And Thank God once again for Maria. She makes having a partly a lot easier.

Christmas 1995

The holidays are getting to be a lot of work for me. I used to look forward to them, but I now seem to get a little bit panicky. I not only do all the shopping and cooking, I need to get the house ready for sleep-overs, too. Alex and his family usually stay the week, and then I have to have New Year's Eve also. I hope I'm strong enough to keep hosting the holidays—at least until my sons get married. And when will that be?

1996

It is difficult to remember all the important things that have happened in 1996—but I'll give it a try.

July 26

We had dad's lobster party. We all had a very rewarding time. The Macarena dance was the hit of the day. Thank God for Maria (who helps with the party); I don't think I could handle all this, by myself anyway.

August

Angela had a beautiful Sweet Sixteen party. She is a truly lovely niece. I adore Doreen and her the same. I wish I had had a daughter like one of my nieces.

August 22, 1996

My Mikey is now twenty-one years old. I always worry about him. I feel he doesn't have enough drive and stamina to survive in this world. He is going out with a lovely girl named Tracy. If I didn't know better, I would say she could be his sister. Isn't it strange how life turns out, that Mike meets someone on the internet who looks so much like him?

December 1996 and January 1997

The Holidays passed this year while I was still in a fog. Dad got very sick in November. Three weeks in the hospital, and he lost thirty pounds.

Alice came to visit and said he only had two weeks more to live. But we celebrated the holidays with him.

March 28

It was difficult not having my twins together for their birthday. I'm having a hard time dealing with Al living in Pittsburg. I miss him very much—he was the one who always talked to me.

April

It is very difficult with Kathy (Joey's girl) not wanting to speak to us. After all these years of us putting up with the crazy things the girl has done, she doesn't want to talk to us any more because Pete called her a bitch. If the shoe fits, I say, wear it. If it doesn't, come talk about it. I guess this is what this girl has striven for all these years—to finally get her Joey all to herself. But I don't feel my son is happy.

May

Alex called me to say he and Tina were going to be engaged, and that she was expecting. I'm thrilled for the two, or should I say the three, of them. I'm going to be a grandmother. (Can't wait!) I'm so happy for Al and Tina, but deep down in my heart there is an open wound for Joe and Kathy. I wish he could be happy, too. Here I am planning a party for my dad's ninetieth birthday, and Al and Tina come up with wedding plans for this August.

My dad was so surprised about the party for him. He thought he was going to an engagement party for Al and Tina. The cocktail party on the veranda was delightful. It was very nice of my dad's neighbors to come. We had a blessing in the chapel for him making ninety and a blessing for Tina and Al, and one for Angela because today was her seventeenth birthday. It was diffi-cult seeing Lenny and Alice at the party and not speaking to each other.

July 27

Tina's shower was today. Her family did a fabulous job having it at the Great Kills Yacht Club. She was so surprised, it was hard to get her to stop crying. She received beautiful gifts, and everyone had a ball. I gave Alex his box of un-derwear and a plaque about him. I hope they will always be happy together.

August 22, 1997

My baby Mike is twenty-two years old today.

Where has the time gone? It seems like it was yesterday when Pete and I brought him home from the hospital. We put him in a dresser drawer with a pillow because we had no furniture. What a treasure he has been all these years.

The wedding is almost here. This is going to be one of the happiest days of my life. I guess into each life a little rain must fall, though, because my brother Ed and Fran cannot make the wedding. He had a heart attack last week and is still in the hospital. He is taking after my mother's side of the family with the arteriosclerosis. First the eyes, and now his heart. I hope the doctors will be able to stop any future attacks to his body.

August 23

Well, here it is—the day I've been waiting for, the day my first-born son Alexander gets married! The house was such a bed of confusion. My brother from Florida, and his family, are staying at my house. The groom is in from Pittsburg and spent his last free night at Dad's. All the ushers looked so handsome in the tuxedos, but the most handsome was the groom. I guess I'm a little bit prejudiced because it is his special day.

I only wish my brother Ed and his wife Fran

could have been here. I also wish my mother, my mother-in-law, and my father-in-law were still alive. They would all have been so happy to see their grandson get married with a mass in Richmond Town's beautiful little church.

Tina looked radiant as she and Howie walked down the isle. I hope to God Al and Tina will always be as happy as they look today. Father Padulla gave a beautiful, and at times funny, service. Mary and I carried down the gifts, and Al and Tina paid a visit to the Blessed Mother's chapel to lay roses at her feet. The church service was one of the most captivating I've ever seen. Now it is off to the Plaza. Wow, what an elegant place. The cocktail hour overlooked Central Park, and the baby lamb chops were delicious. Everyone looked so beautiful and handsome, especially that wonderful father of the groom. I can't believe Pete and I will be married thirty-five years soon.

Now that the wedding is over, we can start looking forward to the baby. I can't believe that Pete and I are going to be grandparents. I'm so excited. I realize that we will always play backseat to her mother and father, but that's natural for a girl to always want to be with her parents. Just as long as we get to see the baby sometimes,

I'll be happy. I can't wait to start buying little presents for him or her.

Tina wanted me to come with her mother and grandmother to see the baby sonogram. It was really kind of her to allow me to be there. It was the most amazing thing to see. I actually saw my little grandson moving around and yawning. Yes, they are going to have a boy. It would be wonderful to have a little Al or Peter, but whatever they decide we will be happy just to have a grandson.

I can't believe the change in Kathy. She is like a different person. She comes in now with a smiling face and kisses everyone. She kids around and actually has conversations with Pete. She now realizes we never meant her harm. I love Joey and want to see him happy. If Kathy is the one for him, then I'll learn to love her, too.

I don't understand why Michael is getting these headaches. I've taken him to a few doctors, and he has had an MRI, and thank God nothing's shown up. But the fact remains that the headaches persist. I'm glad that he has Tracy. She is a very good influence on him. I still feel that they look so much alike that they could be brother and sister. I know I would be very lucky to have Tracy as a daughter-in-law.

November 18

I got a call from my son Alex today. Tina's water broke, and the little guy wants to come out sooner than expected. He is due January 21, so we are just about two months early. They have given her steroids to stop the contractions and medication to speed up the growth of his lungs. I'm very worried. He is only three-and-a-half pounds. I've been saying a lot of prayers that he stays in there a little longer. My first grandchild! Please, God, let him, his mother, and his father all be well.

November 24

Well, the little fella is trying very hard to stay inside his mommy. Tina is remaining in bed in the hospital. Her mother has been there all week, and her sisters were there over the weekend. I told her I would be there for her when she has no one else with her. I miss seeing Alex so much—it has been quite a while. We now have no idea when the baby will make his appearance. It could be a day or another month.

December 5

We finally took a trip to Pittsburg. Mikey drove Joe and me using my car. He is a very good driver. Even around those turns I feel very secure with Mike doing the chauffeuring. We went to Al's plant only to find a note with directions to the hospital. Tina looks very good. She is getting restless, but the little guy is behaving himself and still staying inside his mommy as long as possible. I was so happy to see my son. I hadn't seen Alex since his wedding. He looked kinda stressed out (hardly surprising). I hope his health doesn't get affected by all this stress.

They have a beautiful home—three floors and all the furniture to go with it. I hope they know what they are doing. I hate to see them in a hole before they even get started with life.

Mary smokes an awful lot. I never realized how much until I slept in the house with her smoking. The smell is all over. It was very difficult sleeping with that smell of smoke. I hope she stops, just for her own health.

December 13, 1997

James Joseph Sabatino has arrived. We are now officially grandparents. It's a very different feeling to know my son is now a father. I know he will be a very good daddy. I cannot decide if James looks like Alex or not. He is so small. When we got Joey and Alex, they were almost two months old, and their faces had filled out. James's coloring definitely looks dark, like Tina's. He is so cute. I love him so much already. I can't wait until he starts looking around at us.

December 25

Christmas was very special this year. We have a new life in the family—a little boy who wasn't due until January 21. He came a month and a half early, but thank God he is doing fine.

Pete has been sick ever since we came home from Pittsburg. He has no energy and doesn't even talk. It's almost like living with a zombie. Thank God for my dad and the kids. At least I get some kind of conversation from them.

But it's not the same as having another woman around. Sometimes I miss my mom so much. It's over sixteen years, but to me it's like yesterday. I have no sisters, no daughters, and no one that I really feel especially close to anymore. I get so down in the dumps sometimes. Then I have to think of all the good in my life, and I snap out of it. The latest joy is my little James. I love him so much; I wish I was more expressive, but this is the way that I am. I am always my father's daughter.

January 22, 1998

Now I know what it means to be a grandma. I had to babysit James all day. I had my son's son to feed, change, kiss, and look at for a whole day. I loved every minute of it. Grandpa Al loved holding him, and Grandpa Pete fed him and took pictures.

I had all my girlfriends over, so we had a little shower for Tina. When she came back to pick him up, she opened the gifts. I can't wait for another splendid day like today.

January 25

Another beautiful day: Super Bowl Sunday XXXII. I really wasn't going to do it this year because I felt tired out by the holidays. But Alex wanted to be with us for some kind of holiday because he was in Pittsburg for Christmas and New Year's. We had extra people like Fran, Ed, Jean, Anthony, and a few others. The day was great; everyone brought a dish, and King James was the life of the party. Also Mike, Joe, and Al won the big pots. It was a very fine day for all, especially me!

January 29

Thursday, I went shopping with my little man and his mom. I forgot how difficult it is: taking the stroller out, having the bottle to feed him. Tina was mixing formula on the bench in the mall. Once he ate, he quieted down. Tina exchanged the gorgeous suit Nancy and Bob gave him for a snowsuit for next year. It's hard to imagine such a tiny little baby will fit into this snowsuit. Only time will tell.

January 30

I waited all day for my little angel to come over. But for some reason, Tina wasn't bringing him early. Al missed his early flight, and Pete was very disappointed. He wanted to show his grandson off to his friend on the job. Anyway, we didn't eat dinner until 9:30 at night after Mike went out to Kennedy to pick Al up. My grandson slept over in the cute crib I bought. He is so special. I can't get enough of him. I know I'm the mother-in-law, though, so I must behave!

January 31

The morning was so much fun. Waking up and having baby James in the house is what life is all about. We all had breakfast together and then Tina and Al went shopping. The babysitters were fine. I had to go to Eger, but Pete, Dad, and

Mike had a memorable time holding the little man.

At night we went to brother Ed's party. We are all very lucky to have him celebrating his fifty-ninth birthday.

March 11

The month of February flew by just waiting for little James to come. I feel very fortunate to have a daughter-in-law like Tina. She has brought the baby over so many times these last two weeks. Mostly all the family has now seen James, so I can relax and enjoy him from now on. I think he is beginning to look around and notice people and his surroundings. Babies grow up so fast. He is already over twelve pounds and has a round, pudgy face. I thanked Tina for letting us have him over so often.

I'm still putting my thoughts down into words. I was just thinking about Mike. I wish he was really settled in a good field that he enjoys. He loves to fiddle with the computer and wants to become a programmer. I guess cooking was really not his forte. I only want him to get it all together and be happy. I like Tracy very much, but I know they're very young. They do look really great together.

May 31

I had an unforgettable birthday this year. I can't believe I'm fifty-six. The time has surely flown by. Last night Pete and I went to a supper club with Rose Mary and Ernie. We drank, danced, and laughed all night. Today my family was here, except for Tina, Al, and baby James. I really missed them. My gifts were very special. I guess as the kids get older they really think of Mom a lot. I'm very lucky to have such great sons in my life. My daughter-in-law is also a gem. Kathy and Tracy are very sweet, too.

June

Lou Pederson got married. He looked very happy. Al and his old girlfriend Gloria walked down the aisle together. It was a very strange sight to see. It brought back a lot of memories. Tina was very angry, but I told her, What's the difference? He is your husband and your baby's father now. The past stays in the past.

We had a great time at the reception. I missed Mike and Tracy. He chose not to come because he was starting school.

July 4, 1998

Well, here we are again. The day was beautiful

until around six o'clock, and then the rains came. We had a nice crew over. Rose and John, Ernie and Ro, Larry, Mary and Howie, Barbara and Frank, and all of my family. I loved seeing James in the pool. He loves the water just like his father did. He looks and smiles so much like his father. I could just eat him up, but I was very good—I had to share him with everyone else there.

Tina loves to hang out on Staten Island. I know it's difficult for her. We all like to be near family and friends. When she stays on Staten Island, I do get to see the baby a lot. She's very good that way, as I've said a number of times in these pages. Little James has many people who love him. Sometimes, as I'm gazing into his eyes, I can't believe so many years have gone by. It seems like yesterday when we brought the twins home.

Little Al came to stay with us for two weeks. He was a brave boy to go on the plane by himself. He is such a pleasant and bright child to have around. My brother is very lucky to have such a beautiful son.

July 25

The sun was shining on my dad's lobster party. The entire family was gathered and, as usual, we had a heart-warming time. I hope he lives to be a hundred years old. I know it will be very hard for me when his time is up.

August 6

We arrived in Pittsburg safe and sound. It was wonderful to see my son and his beautiful family. Tina keeps a warm and friendly home. I hope they can make more friends, because it would make life richer for them. I loved having James all to myself for a few days. I had him in bed with Pete and me. I like spending time with my daughter-in-law, too. I wish they were closer to Staten Island.

September

Pete had a stress test done and it didn't turn out so well. It shows that a portion of his heart is not working at normal capacity. He went to NYU for a second opinion, and that doctor advised him to go for the catheterization test. I can't believe that this stage of our lives, seeing so many doctors, has arrived already. We must be getting old. I just keep thinking of my beautiful mother. I hope things will go better for Pete than they did for Mom.

November

We spent Thanksgiving at my brother Ed's

house. We've all had a lot to be thankful for this year. Even though Pete may need bypass surgery, I feel he was at least given a warning to correct the problem. A lot of people just have a heart attack and never recover from it. I still can't believe he had a silent heart attack.

My Joey has been doing a lot of traveling for his job. He recently went to Canada, then Tokyo. He found Japan very expensive. Fourteen hours in a plane must have been a little claustrophobic, too. I worry so much when he flies.

My mind is always on my dear husband lately. If anything happens to him, I don't know how I could go on living. He is my other half. Life needs two parts to survive.

December 6

We celebrated the little man's first birthday. What a day! Tina did a marvelous job planning the party. Alex did a fabulous job paying for it, and we all had a wonderful time enjoying it. The baby didn't cry or get fussy the whole time. He was dancing on my lap to the music. I forgot about Pete's problem for a few hours.

December

Shopping and going to doctors. I feel like

I'm on a merry-go-round and I can't get off. Every time I think of Pete having open heart surgery, I can't help thinking about my mom. She was so positive about the operation. She wanted to be able to walk again without heavy breathing and chest pain. Pete has no symptoms, but all the test show three arteries blocked and a previous heart attack. I just can't lose him to the same kind of surgery: I love him so much.

December 24, 1998

What a fine Christmas Eve. It was beautiful just to have my little man James around. Having a grandchild is as spectacular a feeling as you could get. He is just a pleasure. Fran did a marvelous job with her fish salad, and all my preparation paid off. The only drama was brother Al's plane being four hours late. I felt so bad for Mike and Tracy. He is just such a good kid.

December 25

Christmas Day, and all went well. I was extremely exhausted from all the work, so after James opened his gifts, I went back to bed for three hours. Thank God for Debbie, for getting the house in order and setting the tables again.

When Fran and Eddie got back from Brooklyn, she helped Debbie prepare the spedini. Thank God everyone else cleaned up after the meal too, because I had no energy left at all. The Kaufmans enjoyed the dinner. Ro made a ham, prime rib, mushrooms, and artichokes.

Little James is almost ready to walk. He crawls around very fast and pushes his little telephone walker when he stands up. Sometimes when I look at him I see my son Al, and sometimes I see Tina. I have a feeling that he is not going to be very tall. Those legs look a little shorter than his father's were. How my mother would have enjoyed him, but my father just loves him to death.

My brother's son, Little Al, is a bright and shining star. He is just a delight to have around. I feel very sorry for Allison. She is a very unhappy person. She just doesn't let herself enjoy the surroundings of the moment. I also think she is anorexic. My brother has a big cross on his hands. I told Debbie to seek therapy for her. I hope she is smart enough to listen before it is too late.

Joey is really a boy I could lean on. I always thought Al would be the strong one. But his marriage to Tina has proven that he cannot handle certain things. A mother always wishes the best for her children, and I wish Alex had found a wife who could love and appreciate him the same way I love Pete. I don't feel Tina is doing a proper job as a wife. But I guess I'm old-fashioned and living in the past.

I so enjoy playing Scrabble with Mikey. I feel I taught him well. I find it hard to beat him. He's a great speller. He needs to learn the strategy a little better, and then no one could beat him.

My fourth son, Danny, spent a lot of time in our house. Pete is doing a lot of work for him. Danny works very hard trying to fix up the house. He has a fine wife and mother. Those kids are two gems.

December 31

Well, we all made it to 1999. I feel very lucky to have almost everyone I love here with me to celebrate the new year. We missed Al, Tina, and the little man, and Mary and Howie.

Mike, Tracy, Joe, and Kathy were all here to celebrate. I still wonder if Joe and Kathy will ever marry. They've been together so many years, but there's been no commitment. I love having all my closest friends with us to celebrate.

I'm worried about Pete's surgery.

January 6, 1999

I've taken care of all the paper work for Pete. Now we are waiting for Deborah Hospital to call for an appointment with Dr. McGrath.

I can't even put into words the worry and anxiety I feel about my husband right now. He is still working and claims he feels fine. He still goes in the hot tub. Sometimes at night, I have to listen very closely to make sure he is breathing. I hate living like this. I want my Peter Boy well again.

January 28

Here we all are at Deborah Hospital, waiting for Pete to be brought down to the SICU. The worrying is absolutely incredible. I feel like I'm reliving the past and worrying about my mother making it through the surgery. The nurses are very good keeping us informed about the progress of his surgery. Pretty soon we can go see him.

Peter looked a little frightening the first time we went in. He was still on the respirator and was sleeping. He had all kinds of equipment hooked up to him.

Now a different kind of worry begins. I hope he doesn't run into any complications. He recognized me and the boys. That's a very good sign.

He even said he heard us talking when he was still asleep. My husband was back from his sleep.

January 29

My sons were all with me again. They are such caring boys. It was a great comfort having Rose sleep with me in the room tonight. If anything bad was to happen, I wouldn't have wanted to be alone. Joey is staying with me tonight. He has such a worried look on his face.

January 30

It was wonderful having Joe in the room. We talked about a lot of things. I love him so deeply and wish he could find the same kind of happiness I've had with Pete all these years.

Alex and Mike came in the afternoon. Al has so much tension in his life. I hate giving him more by this worrying about his father. Last night Pete had arrhythmia. But, thank God, after a few hours the medications got his heart rate back in sync again.

Barbara, Frank, Marge, and Tom came to visit Pete last night. I think the company was just a little too much for him.

Today, John and Vinny came in the afternoon. It's hart to tell people not to come.

January 31

I'm so scared that Pete is not going to recover. Every day I come in the morning, I find a new problem. He now has a fever and a low blood count. It sometimes feels like I'm reliving my mother's problems after her surgery. Dr. Sena explained a lot of things to me in his office. I was crying and so upset. He said all these things were common after heart surgery.

February 3

I took my hubby home today. He wanted to stay an extra day, even though the doctor was ready to release him yesterday.

I'm so glad it's all over. Now we just have a little recovering to do, and Mr. Pete will be back in action soon.

April 30

I thought Pete needed just a little recovering. I was very wrong. From the time he was released from Deborah, he spent another twenty-one days in and out of hospitals, treating everything from infections of the leg to whacked-up heart rhythms. I was so scared. A couple of times I thought I was going to lose him. He is my life. Without him I don't know how I could function.

Pete and I have been together almost forty years.

We lost our dear friend John on March 28, the twins' birthday. Of all the days for him to pass away, it had to be on their birthday. Now Rose has to go through life alone. Even though she has children, she will still be alone in that house. At night in bed alone has to be the worst. If she had a daughter, it would make things a little more bearable. Even though I have Pete, sometimes I feel all alone. I guess these are my cards, though, and I have to play the hand as best as I can.

Little James is a treasure for Pete and me. It's the most wonderful feeling in the world to look at your son's child. He has made life more bearable with his big smile. He loves all his little things in our home, and I love to watch him explore. Al and Tina are very lucky to have such a loving healthy boy.

April 9

Pete went into AFib again this morning at 7:00. We called Deborah, and they said to drive down there. It was frightening when they started injecting him with drugs. His pressure was dropping so low, I thought I was going to lose him. He was stabilized Friday, but by Saturday it started in again. This time he was flat lining, and they needed to put a portable pacer on him, with paddles in the front and back to zap him when his heart paused for too long. Thank God Jeanie and Anthony, Joey and Kathy, and Rose were there. It's times like these you need your loved ones around you. On Monday they put a pacemaker in him. We hope all the problems are behind us, but the doctor said to cancel our trip to Spain. Pete was very disappointed.

Marge and Tom, and Pete and I, went to Hanley's condo at the shore. After five minutes, we called an ambulance. We thought Pete was having a heart attack: chest pains, gray in the face, and cold sweats. I rode in the front seat and cried my eyes out. The pressure has really been a lot for me. I was so scared, but I never let Pete see me like that. It turned out to be gastric, thank God.

July 10

Another mild AFib incident.

July 24

Another lobster party! Dad has now reached the age of ninety-two. It's wonderful to have all my family together, especially my three sons and little man James. He loves the water, and he's such a smart little boy. I loved having Lil' Al for the week. He reminds me so much of my brother Al. So much energy and laughing all the time.

August 7

We had James over today. He absolutely loves to play the piano. I now have a little piano for him and a big one for me.

He came over a couple more times this week. Tina has been a real doll in letting us enjoy him. I hope she and Al start to have things a little easier. He needs a job back in New York. James says so many words for a one-and-a-half-year-old. He speaks very clearly in his one-word sentences.

October 30

Oh, what a splendid day! I have a new grandson, Nicholas Michael Sabatino. I'm so proud of Al and Tina. She had a really difficult delivery, but now they have a beautiful little boy—eight pounds and eight ounces. He has very light skin and blue eyes. He is nursing, which I know is the best thing for him. I can't wait to visit with all of them.

December 25

I worked so hard to have a rewarding Christmas Eve with all the people I love. Everything went well, except that Al and Tina and the baby were sick. I was so looking forward to the baby being here in the morning, but Tina felt it was better to be at her mother's house. I can't blame her, but it still hurts to know I can never have any one of my children to care that way about me and want to be with Pete and me. I never realized, when the boys were little, how empty inside I would feel when they grew up. I know they all love us, but it is not the love of a daughter caring about her mom and dad.

Pete did all the gift calling, and everything went smoothly. I wished the lawyer Salvatore would dress a little. The holidays are so festive, and he always looks terrible.

Christmas Day was delightful. I was very tired from the night before, so to have just five for dinner was a blessing. I set the dining room beautiful and we ate around 5:00 p.m. Kathy and Joey were a pleasure to have with us. Mike went to Tracy's. Tina stayed at her mother. I was so grateful to have my wonderful husband laughing and celebrating Christmas with me. Every time I think of all that he went through and a few times almost losing him, it makes me realize how lucky we are to have each other.

I have so many fine men in my life, including a beautiful grandson. He came over on Sunday but was still sick. He didn't even enjoy opening his presents. I felt so bad for my little dolly.

So we all had a wonderful Christmas Eve this year. No late planes. No crying babies. No sicknesses. It was just beautiful. But it was a tremendous amount of work. We had to put three tables in the dining room. I never felt so tired in my life. I suppose I'm getting a little older. I wish some day I'll be able to go to my children's houses for a holiday. James really enjoyed Santa Claus, who was played by Michael again. He does such a good job as Santa. All the kids just loved him. Next year Nicholas will be able to enjoy the festivities. Dad gave everyone a very large envelope this year. I think it's great that at ninety-three he still enjoys giving everyone a gift.

New Year's Eve 2000 was a little quiet this year. I was totally wiped out from Christmas and my brother Al's family was staying with us for the entire week.

I set the bar with a tablecloth, candles, good china and crystal, and a delightful meal. My hus-

band, my Dad and I brought in 2001.

Two years ago today Peter was having his open heart surgery. Two years just flew by. I thank god every day for letting me have my husband with me.

Baby Nicholas was baptized today. The ceremony was beautiful. Michael made a good-looking godfather. It was very nice having it in Pittsburg. Then we celebrated Super Bowl XXXV at Al and Tina's house with both immediate families. I missed Kathy not being with us.

January 2000

Well, we all made it to the new millennium. I know it actually will be 2000 years next year, but the world wanted to celebrate this year, so we had to go with the flow.

Pete and I had a great New Year's Eve party, with a few friends and some of their children and grandchildren. I missed not have my sons here. (I actually mean I wish my sons could have celebrated with us.)

We have so much to be thankful for: the start of the new thousand years. My husband's health is excellent. My dad couldn't be better, and all the boys. Tina, Kathy, and Tracy are in good health. And we have a marvelous little man called James. I know he is going to be very bright. He talks up a storm and still likes the piano.

I loved the whole party, but I couldn't stop thinking about Rose. She wanted to stay home all alone. Maybe I would feel the same way. I hope I never find out. I hope I'm the one to go first. I think it must be just awful to climb into an empty bed at night. I hope one day Rose will meet someone else and make a new life for herself.

February 1, 2001

Mark Zogby died today. I couldn't believe it. I heard he died of liver cancer. I know he couldn't accept his brother Matthew's death. I hope he is now at peace with himself. His mother was so distraught; I don't want to ever know how she feels. I pray to God he takes me before any of my children.

February-March

Pete and I had a beautiful Florida vacation. After all these years, we can still laugh together. It's so important to love each other and be able to laugh and do happy things together. It's really amazing that you don't even have to spend a lot of money. As long as we have each other, I know we'll both be happy.

March

On our way back to New York from Florida, we stopped in Georgia to visit with my cousin Petey. Jean was also there this year. We enjoyed each other's company and had a satisfying few days together. Pete and I love to shop at Harry's fish market. I feel a kid in a candy store with such a large selection of great foods to cook.

March 28

It was really nice having the twins together for their birthday. It's hard to believe that thirty-two years have already passed. It seems like only yesterday we picked them up from the adoption agency. We were so thrilled and happy to be able to have two babies to love, and believe me I've loved them so much for the past thirty two years.

June 9, 2001

Twenty years ago today, my beautiful mother died. I still miss her very much today. The pain is gone, but I'll always miss her presence. I had a mass said at the convent in Richmond Town, and my dad and I went. I can hardly believe I still have my father to talk to, and believe me, he can talk. We argue a lot, but we love each other.

We went away this weekend to the Goldin Inn. I'm in Avalon, New Jersey. All our friends came along. It seems as if every time Pete and I make plans to go to a new place, the whole gang comes along. We had so much fun with each other. It was a big-band weekend. The price was right, the company was the best, and Pete and I had a thoroughly enjoyable time.

July 20

We had my dad's lobster party earlier this year. His birthday is actually on the 26th, when he will be ninety-four. Oh, my, what a fantastic man. He sings, eats, drinks, talks, laughs, and makes everyone around him happy. Everyone in the family came. I worry about Pete having to do so much work with the lobsters. Thank God the men go down and help him.

The Hamptons were a wonder this year. The weather was just superb. I love shopping in Southampton. They have a great thrift store there. It's fun to shop in those kinds of ritzy thrift stores.

We had lunch with Cookie. I'm happy and grateful that we were able to put things aside and spend a little time together. But it wasn't the same. We were so close at one time; now it feels like there is a wall between us.

August 2001

We had a block party for the first time in about twenty-five years. It was a lot of fun, and nice to meet all the new neighbors. I invited a lot of people. I was so exhausted by the end of the night. I guess being fifty-nine is catching up to old age. I can't seem to do what I used to. I force myself to do everything, but then I'm so tired afterwards. James and Nicholas had a gleam in their eyes. James really enjoyed the day. I was sorry they came late, but the kids had moved back from Pittsburg the day before. I'm happy that they are going to live here now but sad the way things happened. My son had a partner from hell. I'll never understand why people can be so rotten.

September 11, 2001

It seems like the world stopped rotating today. Our life as we know it will never be the same.

I was working for elections at PS 23 when my friend Kim got a phone call from her husband in

Hoboken. He said a plane had hit the Twin Towers. We all thought it was a freak accident. I called Pete and told him to put the TV on. Fifteen minutes later, Kim's husband called again and said a second plane had hit the other tower. Now we knew the U.S. was under some kind of attack. It was a sickening feeling. When she said the tower was collapsing, I started to cry. All I could think of were the thousands of people dying in that horrible way. And then I was worried about Joey and Michael. I knew that they worked in Manhattan. We had no TV at the school, so we couldn't see what was happening. I wanted to be home with my family in the worst way. I knew Alex wasn't working, though, so I had one less to worry about. I called Pete around noon and learned from him that Mike and Joe were safe. So many young people had died for no good reason.

October 10, 2002

Dad died a very peaceful death at the age of ninety-five.

February 2003

It's like time stood still after 9/11. Now I can start to write again. While Pete and I were in

Florida, he started getting the chills and a high fever. It was very frightening, because I couldn't do anything for him. We went to a place called The Villages. The town square was the nicest part of it. I had to call the EMS for Pete because of the fever.

March 2003

We came back to New York from Florida, and then Pete's fever started to come again every day. Went to SIUH for a week with no results.

August 2003

Another week in SIUH came and went with no results. The doctors sent Pete home and said that, usually after ninety days, these things go away. He was taking prednisone to ease the effects of the fevers.

During all this time, our life was a mess. I couldn't even enjoy my two dear grandchildren. In July, things got very bad. Pete was so weak all the time. I knew he was dying. I wrote a letter to a doctor at Cornell Medical Center. We went to see Dr. Jason Kendler. He took a blood culture and, four days later, told us he was admitting him to Cornell because he had raging infections in his blood. After forty days in that Manhattan hos-

pital, Pete came home cured. Now we could get our life back together again.

March 6, 2004

A beautiful little princess came into our lives. We were driving home from Florida when we got a call from our son Alex that we now had a granddaughter, Annie Rose. I was so thrilled to finally have a little girl in my life. She looks just like Al—very fair, with light eyes. Li'l Nickie is a little jealous, but James is like a little daddy.

August 9, 2005

I don't know where the time goes. I seem to write less and less. I guess it must be the sixties; I still can't believe I am sixty-three and collecting my Social Security checks.

We now have two gorgeous granddaughters. Michael got married on March 18, and Li'l Isabella arrived on June 5, 2005.

It was so special to be at the hospital when Enrica was in labor. This was the first grandchild we were able to be at the hospital for. Mike was so proud-looking. He will make the best daddy. He was always great with babies. I can't believe he has one of his own.

If Joey gets married and has a child, I feel my life will be complete. Thank God Pete has been healthy. I always ask God for small increments of good health for all my family and friends.

We lost my two cousin Lennies this past year. Lenny Saparata died last August at Lake Tahoe of heart trouble. It was expected. But Lenny Impastato died on a tennis court in Cancun last Thanksgiving Day. I still can't believe he is dead. He seemed the healthiest of all the cousins, and now he is gone. I really miss him. He was cremated in Cancun; all we had was a memorial service. It was attended by all his friends and family except for his first and second wives. It was ironic that neither wife could attend. I'm going to write more often.

June 5, 2006

Little Isabella is one year old today. Oh, she looked so beautiful in her fancy dress. I feel like I've bonded the closest to her of all my grandchildren. I suppose taking care of her in our home makes the difference. I love all my grandchildren equally, but Isabella is very special. She has a bodacious quality. Pete and I were given another chance to enjoy a baby again.

June 9

It is now twenty-five years since my mom died. Sometimes it seems like yesterday. I still miss her tremendously. Maybe if I had a daughter to confide in, I'd feel differently. Sometimes I get so depressed about not being able to talk to anyone about my feelings. I love my husband and my boys with all my heart, but they can't and don't understand a woman. I wish my Joey could be happy with a wife and kids. Before I join my mom, that's what I want to see most.

Christmas Eve 2006

I am so lucky to have all my immediate family with us except for Li'l Al and my brother. Since they came up for Thanksgiving, and we ate together at Fran and Eddie's, I guess Christmas was not on the agenda. I can't believe after all these years I have never missed a Santa Claus for the Eve. All the kids were excited. It's hard to believe that our nine-year-old James still believes. Annie, Bel, and Nickie were all thrilled at the sight of the man in the red suit. I'm glad I stopped the gifts to and from Ed's family and Danny and Rachel. It just had gotten to be too much for me.

I wish my dad was still here. He was such a

big help with the cooking. I miss having our special conversations.

February-March 2007

I love being at the Tides in Hollywood Beach. We had an especially nice time when Bob and Nancy came down. It was fun having them stay at the Marriot only one block away. Pete gets to play golf with Carl, and I get to shop and do a lot of water, reading, and beach walking. I regret, though, that we get to miss our Annie's birthday every March 6.

March 28

The twins are thirty-eight. Nearly forty years, and it seems like barely a week's gone by since we went to pick up those two bundles of joy. They have given us such pleasure all these years. Al has given us extra joy for James, Nickie, and Annie Rose. We are so lucky to have loving grandchildren. I still get the biggest kick out of Isabella, because I see her so often. She is very bright and loving.

June 5, 2007

Isabella is a bright shining star for just two years old. She has more than a fifty-word vocab-

ulary. I see so much of Michael in her eyes. She can be very pensive when she wants to be.

March 29, 2008

It seems the older I get the faster time goes by. My dad always told me how fast life passes you by; now I know from my own experience. Joe and Al have reached thirty-nine. My grandchildren now number five. Annalisa was born while we were in Florida, on February 27. Michael has another lovely daughter. This one looks exactly like Michael's baby pictures.

I need to write more often.

July 31, 2008

I'm glad I said I would write more often, but it seems as if the days just roll right into one another. When I was in my teens, I wrote almost every day. Oh, how delightful it seemed to be able to put my thoughts on paper. Now I find it difficult to gather the right thoughts to put down. I thank God every day for the life he has given me. Pete and I have had thirty-five blessed years together. Don't get me wrong, we've had our ups and downs, and sickness, too. But most of the time we've laughed, made love, had our children, traveled, entertained, and now God has let us enjoy our grandchildren. Annalisa is five months old. She now is a combo, but she has such a chunky body that all you want to do is hug her. We just finished another lobster party. Dad, you would have enjoyed all the new grandchildren! We are all so happy that Joey is going to have a baby. His girlfriend Osmara is a sweet and warm girl. I like her very much. I hope their life together will bring them as much happiness as Pete and I have had together these forty-five years.

January 23, 2009

It has been a long time since I jotted down any thoughts. I have a new grandchild. He lives in Miami, and his name is Joseph Sabastian Sabatino. A beautiful baby he is. Always laughing. He looks just like his dad, with a tinge of his mom.

Christmas was delicious with all my children and grandchildren. Osmara has an eleven-year-old daughter named Sophia. She calls us Gramma and Grandpa. I guess I now have seven grandchildren. I'm writing in my room with Belle and Annalisa running around up here. They are the cutest things and they're very good. But they also wear me out. I'm glad I feel a lot better now. The doctor added more meds for my blood pres-

sure. I hope it stays regulated. I felt pretty sick during the month of December.

March 30, 2010

I don't understand why it takes me so much time between my writing sessions. Pete and I have had our little bouts of sickness, but nothing major. He gets that coughing and congestion, but since we went to Florida this year, he's been better. I hope he doesn't need sinus surgery. It scares me that he would have to stop the Plavix and aspirin for almost twenty days. The twins are now forty-one years old. Joey's son is so cute. He seems just like his father did at that age. We had lots of fun in the pool in Florida with the baby. He splashes so much water in his face and doesn't cry. I miss my other grandchildren, especially Anna, because she is the one we take care of three days a week now. I have a special place for Belle in my heart. And Annie Rose will always be my first granddaughter. I thank God every day for giving me such a good life. I have so much love for all my family. I hope I will be around a long time so I can share it with them.

September 21, 2010

Well, Li'l Jo-Jo is two years old today. He

looks and acts just like his daddy. I wish he lived a little closer so I could kiss and squeeze him more often. Osmara seems like the right gal for Joey. It took long enough for him to make up his mind. I'm glad they are having another baby and Jo-Jo will have a brother.

Anna has been talking so much better. She still seems to stutter, but she is getting her points across. She always tells me, "I love you, Nana." Belle once told me she wished she could be inside me because she loves me so much. It's like I have my own little daughters now that I'm sixty-eight.

We went to Al and Tina's the other day to see the kids. They only live a half hour away, but it seems like we never see them. The last time was for Pete's and Mikie's birthday on August 22— Pete was seventy, and Mike thirty-five. I had a party for Pete with just friends, and three-quarters of our friends didn't make it. I felt so bad for Pete.

Annie Rose is getting very pretty. After we are there a while, she warms up and gets close to me. The other guys are boys, as usual.

The dog makes us crazy. He just keeps barking and barking. Alex was in so much pain with his back, he looked crooked. I really miss not seeing them as much as we used to, but the kids *constantly have games to play. I guess things were the same when our boys were growing up.*

The lobster party in July was another success. It was so much work but loads of fun.

October 30, 2010

Matthew Peter Sabatino was born today. He was born the same day as Nickie, only ten years later. That's quite a coincidence, that Alex's second son and Joey's second son were born on the same day. I'm so happy that Joey has two sons of his own. They are both particularly cute. Li'l Matt looks just like his brother, only a little darker. I wish we could see the baby, but I just can't do another plane trip. We just got back from Sedona, Arizona. It was one of the finest places I've ever seen. The red mountains and vast open spaces are just breathtaking. We had a very satisfying vacation. Pete and I always have great times on vacation. I love being just the two of us. I know one of these days one of us will be alone. I hope and pray it won't be for a long time to come.

Thanksgiving 2010

We spent the day at Mike and Enrica's. They have a small house, but there is always plenty to eat and lots of good company. Just being with my Belle and Anna make the day special.

Saturday the family was all together at Eddie and Fran's. Again, plenty of food and good company. We haven't spent a Thanksgiving with Al and Tina, so it was great having Annie Rose, James, Nickie. Li'l Julianna is such a treasure. She has a great personality and is the friendliest child there. I missed my Joey and his family, but I guess we can't have everything perfect all the time.

December 24, 2010

Christmas Eve at the Sabatinos' was great as usual. Everyone was here except for my Joey and his family. Baby Matt hasn't gotten his shots yet, so he can't fly on a plane. I hope next year we can all be together. I feel I'm getting older and don't know how long I can do all this cooking and partying. I was in a lot of pain when I went to bed.

December 27, 2010

Boy, what a massive snowfall we had. I think we got over two feet. We can't even get out of our house. I haven't seen this much snow in a very long time. I wish I was in Florida right now, because I really don't enjoy the snow anymore. There was a time I loved going out to make snowmen and loved to ski. Now I think I would rather be in Florida, where Joey is.

March 20, 2011

We are now heading up to Atlanta, Georgia. We spent one of the best winters this year. Every day, the sun was out and we were in the pool. We saw lots of friends and my two grandsons. They are so much a pleasure. We had the whole crew come over every Saturday and Sunday. It was a lot of work, what with all the cooking, but I loved seeing my Joey and the kids.

Sophia seems to be improving a bit. I hope, as she gets older, she will be able to socialize more.

Peter and Jean look great. I can't believe Peter's throat cancer was cured. They still plan on separate lives as soon as they can sell the house. I feel it is such a foolish thing to do at this stage in life. Peter still hasn't heard from Provie. I can't understand her anymore.

April 24, 2011–Easter

We all had a superb time together. I had all my children and grandchildren around me.

Again, it was a lot of work but well worth it. Just having my three sons together—and of course the fourth one, Danny, and his family came. Li'l Danielle loves me like a gramma and I feel she's like my first granddaughter. Alex was kinda quiet for the day. I guess he has a lot on his mind, what with the new businesses. I hope everything goes will for him; he deserves a break. Joey works way too hard. I hope someday his business will afford him some quality time off. It was great having him and his family for six days. Lots of extra work but worth it. Li'l Joe and Matthew are such treasures. I hope Mike goes back to work soon. I worry about him, Enrica, and the girls.

July 5, 2012

I can't believe it's been over a year since I last wrote in this book. My dad always told me, as I've said before in this diary, that the older you get, the faster time rushes by. It was a good year for me and my whole family. My son Alex finally left Lenny Pirrello. I'm sorry that Lenny was never able to see the hard-working individual he had working for him.

I know Alex will do well with whatever he does. The kids have grown so fast. Annie Rose had her first communion in April. She looked so beautiful. The ceremony at her church was the best I've ever seen for receiving a sacrament.

Christmas was just as much fun as usual. Sometimes I think this will be the last year I'll have Eddie, Fran, and their kids, but then I do it again.

Now we're waiting for the lobster party. Everyone is so looking forward to it.

Isabella had her seventh birthday just after my seventieth. I can't believe I'm really seventy. I know I look and feel it, but I just can't accept it. I get so tired simply doing my work around the house, but I guess that's the reward of a senior citizen. I love all my children, my husband, and my grandchildren so much. I hope I can stay around to see them all grow up.

Pete and I have had a very, very happy life together. I hope we can get a lot more years to enjoy. I'm looking forward to spending time at the condo we bought in Florida. I know Joey enjoys going there to get some peace and quiet. I can't wait to see Li'l Jo-Jo and Matthew Peter. Another month, and we'll all be together, if God wishes, for the annual lobster party.

May 4, 2017

I'm married fifty-four years today. My life with Pete has mostly been filled with happiness.

We have loved each other for so long. We raised three wonderful boys whom I love so very much, and then came the grandchildren. How could two people who could not conceive their own biological child have been so blessed!

My grandchildren mean the world to me. I love watching them become admirable adults. So far my James is in college. Nick is a great baseball high school player. Annie Rose loves her cheerleading. Isabella loves everyone and enjoys her school and track. Anna is a whiz on the track. She just flies through the air. Jo-Jo is such a happy little boy with everyone and everything he does. He really loves football. Little Matthew, my youngest of the crew, very much enjoys music. He has such rhythm when he dances. And he's enamored of his sweets. Sophia I hope will blossom into a striking woman. She graduates high school this year, and I hope all goes well for her. She is a great little artist. So you see, I know and love all my grandchildren, and I thank God every day for sending them to me.

September 21, 2019

Today is my Jo-Jo's birthday. He is eleven. They grow too fast, and I'm getting old too fast. Sometimes I wish I could turn back the clock. I think the happiest time in my life was my thirties. The boys were all young, and Pete and I had so many parties. Life has been good to us. God sending us our three little boys was the greatest gift He could have given us.

Thank God for Mike. He helped us make our Sabatino tomato sauce. We couldn't have done it without him. Thank you, Alex, for bringing us those beautiful crates of tomatoes, and I thank my little Bel, Anna, and Enrica for helping out, too.

Pete fell down and landed on his face. He looks like a racoon. He fell on Friday, and Saturday we made the sauce.

I had a new hip put in on June 26. The doctor said it's fabulous now, and I feel great.

I had hand surgery on September 18 and was able to write three days later.

Bel started St. Joe's, and Nicky started college. I can't believe how grown up all my grandchildren are.

My best friend Rose went through some pretty rough surgery a few months back. She really is a fighter. She has gotten to look like a little old lady with white hair. But she is still my strong Rosie.

I miss friends and family who have passed

away. But that's how life has to be. I hope Pete and I have a long time to be here.

March 2020

And so now we have the coronavirus, more commonly know as Covid-19, the disease it causes. So many people are getting sick and dying. There is no cure yet. My son Alex caught the virus and is in the hospital. I have not been this upset before. I can't do anything to help him. He has blood clots in his lungs. His spleen is enlarged, a high enzyme count in his liver, and heart involvement. Oh, please, God take care of my son.

I still feel so bad about finding out about Mike and Enrica's separation. He says they just grew apart. I think it is terrible for the girls. I was so happy that Mike brought them to Florida this year. They had a lot of fun. They played in the waves.

August 2020

My son Alex is still being tested for the residual effects of the virus. I pray all his problems will get better. He has gone through so much adversity in his life—bad business deals and too much debt with his house and expenses in his life.

Thank God all my grandchildren are fine. My oldest grandchild, James, became a nurse, and I'm very proud of him. Annie Rose is now sixteen. And my dear Peter Boy is going to be eighty this month.

My son Joey has been learning to play piano. It calms him down from his stressful job. He is living in a gorgeous home that overlooks a golf course. All I want is for my sons to be happy. Pete and I have had such a good life; I wish the same for them.

September 11, 2020

It has been nineteen years since that terrible day that killed three thousand people. It is something I shall never forget.

6

FULL CIRCLE

THE YELLOW ROSES ON MY MOTHER'S GRAVE glistened in the bright sunlight. My heart was overwhelmed with happiness, and I still felt pangs of sadness. If only I could speak to her! I thought. I would tell her that her youngest son Alexander had finally gotten married.

I can remember her asking, "Alex, when are you going to get married?" Year after year passed, yet my brother remained single. He traveled around the world during his forty-two years of bachelorhood. Spending two years in Vietnam and two in Thailand gave him a voracious appetite for women of all ages. I suppose that might have been one of the reasons he stayed single for so long.

One day about four years ago, I received a phone call from him. He said that he had finally found the right woman, and he wanted to get married soon. He and his fiancée lived in Florida, but they wanted the ceremony to take place in New York City. He asked me to plan the whole event, from the church to the reception. It was a big undertaking, since I only had two months to pull it all together.

I cried in the church as I looked around at all the radiant faces. They were happy tears for my brother and bittersweet ones because my mother was not there to see the event finally taking place.

During the reception, I was asked to dance with my brother. We held each other tight. Our eyes met as we whirled around the room to the music of "One Moment in Time," tears welled up in both our eyes as we danced. Our thoughts were as one. I was taking my mother's place. . .and we danced and danced.

CPSIA information can be obtained
at www.ICGtesting.com
Printed in the USA
BVHW080519090321
602009BV00005B/744